D O U B T

DOUBT

TRUSTING
GOD'S
PROMISES

ELYSE FITZPATRICK

P&R

PUBLISHING

P.O. BOX 817 • PHILLIPSBURG • NEW JERSEY 08865-0817

Printed in the United States of America

Library of Congress Cataloging-in-Publication Data

Names: Fitzpatrick, Elyse, 1950- author.
Title: Doubt : trusting God's promises / Elyse Fitzpatrick.
Description: Phillipsburg : P&R Publishing, 2018. | Series: 31-day
  devotionals for life | Includes bibliographical references.
Identifiers: LCCN 2018033676| ISBN 9781629953663 (pbk.) | ISBN 9781629953670
  (epub) | ISBN 9781629953687 (mobi)
Subjects: LCSH: Faith--Prayers and devotions.
Classification: LCC BV4637 .F49 2018 | DDC 234/.23--dc23
LC record available at https://lccn.loc.gov/2018033676

Contents

Tips for Reading This Devotional

EARLY IN OUR MARRIAGE, my wife and I lived on the top floor of a town house, in a small one-bedroom apartment. Whenever it rained, leaks in the roof would drip through the ceiling and onto our floors. I remember placing buckets in different parts of the apartment and watching the water slowly drip, one drop at a time. I put large buckets out and thought, *It'll take a while to fill them.* The water built up over time, and often I was surprised at how quickly those buckets filled up, overflowing if I didn't pay close enough attention.

This devotional is just like rain filling up a bucket. It's slow, and it builds over time. Just a few verses every day. Drip. Drip. Drip. Just a few drops of Scripture daily to satiate your parched soul.

We start with Scripture. God's Word is powerful. In fact, it's the most powerful force in the entire universe.[1] It turns the hearts of kings, brings comfort to the lowly, and gives spiritual sight to the blind. It transforms lives and turns them upside down. We know that the Bible is God's very own words, so we read and study it to know God himself.

Our study of Scripture is practical. Theology should change how we live. It's crucial to connect the Word with your struggles. Often, as you read this devotional, you'll see the word *you* because Elyse speaks directly to you, the reader. You'll get much more from this experience if you answer her questions and follow her practical suggestions. Don't skip them. Do them for the sake of your own soul.

Our study of Scripture is worshipful. Fundamentally, any struggle with doubt is a worship problem. We've lost our orientation toward the One who should rule our lives, and we need to turn back to him. The Word points us to Christ, who rescues us from our doubt and reorients our life. The goal of your time in God's Word should always be worship. As you grow in your affections for Christ, the King, you learn to do battle with your doubts. As Elyse teaches, doubt is normal for Christians. But just because you struggle with doubt doesn't mean that your life is hopeless. Christ can lead you through your doubts—and to faith in him. Adore Christ. Love him. Cherish him. Praise him. Honor him. Give your whole life to him. Don't hold anything back.

If you find this devotional helpful (and I trust that you will!), reread it in different seasons of your life. Work through it this coming month, and then come back to it a year from now, to remind yourself how to do battle with your doubts.

This devotional is *not* meant to be a comprehensive guide to fighting doubt. Good volumes are already written for that purpose. Buy them and make good use of them. You'll see several resources listed at the end of the book.

That's enough for now. Let's begin.

Deepak Reju

Introduction

IF THERE'S ONE thing that I've learned throughout my decades of interacting with Christians, it's this: everyone has doubts about their faith . . . *even me.* My guess is that you're reading this devotional right now because you're struggling with doubt yourself, and perhaps it feels overwhelming. Perhaps you're new to this walk of faith and you still have nagging questions—or you're wondering whether you were maybe a bit hasty in buying into this new life.

Or maybe, like me, you've been a Christian for decades, but you still wonder things such as: Is all this Christianity stuff really—I mean *really*—true? Is God who he says he is in the Bible? For that matter, is the Bible really God's Word? Or, even assuming that the Bible is God's Word, maybe I've been reading it wrong or making assumptions that I shouldn't have made—like assuming that God will save me when that's not the case. Am I really forgiven, or am I just kidding myself?

And then there's the whole problem of the way my life has played out. If God is really the all-powerful, all-wise, all-loving God he declares himself to be, then why isn't my life (my marriage, family, job, ministry, health, or bank account) what I hoped it would be? Have I misjudged or misunderstood God? Why do I continue to struggle with my own sin and failures?

At the bottom of all these "whys" is one more, really big one: *Why am I still struggling to believe?* Aren't I supposed to have the rock-solid conviction of faith that the people in the Bible (and my leaders) seem to have? Does my struggle to believe prove that my faith isn't genuine and that I shouldn't count on any kind of blessing from God? *Am I just fooling myself?*

I know the kinds of questions that doubters ask because I've asked, *and many times continue to ask*, every one of them myself. Sure, I've been a Christian for nearly half a century (wow—that seems like a long time!), but I still question. *Really? Is it really true?* I still wake up in the middle of the night and wonder if God really loves me and will take care of _____ the way I hope he will. In addition, I've known many people of faith who looked pretty good on the surface but who really struggled in private, too. From those interactions, I've learned that I'm not alone in my doubting. Neither are you. In fact, though it may seem counterintuitive, the Bible is chock-full of men and women who were known as people of faith but who also doubted, just like we do. In fact, some of them even doubted while they were conversing with God himself.

Why is doubt so ubiquitous? Why do we all have so much trouble with certainty? Not surprisingly, the Bible gives us the reason. We all struggle against doubt because "we walk by faith, not by sight" (2 Cor. 5:7).

We are physical creatures on a physical earth. Much of what we know, we know through our physical bodies. We are used to gaining certainty through our physical senses. For instance, at this moment, I am sensing a computer on my lap. I feel the aluminum casing with my wrists. I am touching the plastic keys and hearing the click-click as I structure my thoughts into sentences. I see the screen—its many colors and the way it signals me when I've made an error or stopped typing. I feel the warmth of the fan in the casing as it rests on my lap. I am certain my laptop is here. How do I know? I can touch it—there's no faith involved. Right now, as far as my writing process is concerned, I'm walking *by sight* and *not by faith*. When you think about it, that's the primary way that we know anything. I experience the world around me, and I know that it's there.[1]

But that's not the only way that I know what I know. I know many things because I've been taught them. For instance, I've studied the Civil War—and, though I didn't witness it firsthand,

10

I know without doubt that it was an actual event. Sure, I've seen some pictures and visited many battlefields, but that wouldn't prove that it happened without the reliable testimony of those who were there. I've seen artifacts such as letters, newspapers, and the texts of political speeches that assure me that what I'm learning is true. This is how we discover so much of what we know. By the same token, I know that *Voyager* has traveled to the outer limits of our solar system because I've been to the Jet Propulsion Laboratory in Pasadena and seen evidence. I've seen a life-sized model, pictures of the men and women who built it, and the transcription of the messages it has sent back. When it comes to history, science, mathematics, geography, and ancient and modern world cultures, I know what I know mostly because I believe credible witnesses who either were there or have gained extensive knowledge through study. In each of these areas, I put aside doubt (mostly) because I have no reason not to.

Superficial belief in others' testimony about things that we haven't personally witnessed is normal and commonplace. But religious faith is in a different category, isn't it? Perhaps such faith feels like an untethering of our reason. We wonder if our Christianity is just a mindless *leap of faith*. Or is there enough eyewitness evidence to push us beyond unbelief?

We all struggle with inward doubts that arise even when we have strong evidence to convince us. In such cases, doubt occurs for two reasons: First of all, the truth about who I am, and who God is, is *way* more important than whether *Voyager* is actually a grand hoax. Everything in this life and the life to come (if there is one) is riding on it. Second, because we are prone to unbelief by nature, doubt is just part of our DNA. Face it: we are, all of us, Doubting Thomases.

In the readings that follow, you'll meet famous Bible characters who doubted, find evidences to bolster your faith, and enjoy the promises that God has made to those who feel like they have only microscopic faith (smaller than a mustard seed). In addition, every devotional has two takeaway truths for you to memorize or write out in order to help you when you feel condemned because of your doubt. These truths are also found on pages 87–92.

Above all else, though, we want you to know that you're not alone. Doubter, you are welcome here.

DOUBTERS
IN THE BIBLE

DAY 1

A Doubter in Paradise

Now the serpent was more crafty than any other beast
of the field that the LORD God had made. He said to the
woman, "Did God actually say . . . ?" (Gen. 3:1)

INTO THEIR SPLENDID garden home, a place where "Are
you really telling me the truth?" had never once been thought, let
alone asked, the beguiling serpent hissed his foul question: "Did
God actually say, 'You shall not eat of any tree in the garden?'"
(Gen. 3:1)

In that moment, at the beginning of the history of our race,
Satan introduced doubt into the heart of the woman. That phrase,
"Did God actually say?" has echoed down through millennia.
Through centuries of permutations, it has whispered, "Is there a
God? Does he speak? Does the God of the Bible really exist? Is
the Bible actually God's Word? Is his way *really* the right way?"
And, more personally, "Is God actually speaking to me? Does he
know and care about me? Am I his? Am I loved? Can I trust him?"

If Eve and Adam had resisted Satan, you and I wouldn't struggle with doubt the way we do. But they didn't, so we question
and wonder and struggle. To make things worse, we think that
we're alone in this battle. We look around at other Christians who
seem confident and filled with faith, and we think we are some-
how different. Maybe our faith is intrinsically flawed . . . or maybe
we don't really belong in God's family.

We're revisiting the story of the first temptation today because
I want to remind you that you're not alone in your doubts. Doubt
has been with us since the very beginning—since our first parents
fell and were exiled from paradise. At some point they probably
began to doubt whether they used to walk with the Lord in the

"cool of the day" (Gen. 3:8). From their exile onward, we have all had to walk by faith, not by sight. We have had to try to *see* "him who is invisible" (Heb. 11:27), as Moses did—and, though there were occasions when Moses did that well, there were also other times when he failed miserably and was engulfed with doubt. None of us have had the certitude that Adam and Eve knew. All of us struggle.

Remembering that doubt has been a part of the human experience since the beginning is meant to bring you comfort; it is meant to silence the inner accuser who tells you that you're different from everyone else. Today I want you to know that you are not alone. Every daughter and son of faith has also been a child of doubt, as you will soon see. But, for today, let me encourage you to think about these truths and to ask God to help you remember. Walking by faith, striving to see what our natural eyes cannot see, is impossible on our own. *But we're not alone.* He is with us.

If you can, take time now to list the four or five most troubling thoughts that you have. Next, in prayer, ask the Lord to help you find answers to them as we study together. Remember—we're not striving for complete certainty here. One of Satan's big lies is to tell you that, if you don't have complete certainty, you're doubting—and that God hates doubters. That's a lie. God promised salvation to the first two doubters (see Gen. 3:15) . . . and he has salvation for you, too.

Truth 1: Doubt has been around since the beginning.

Truth 2: God loves and saves doubters.

DAY 2

The Doubting Father of Our Faith

Then Abraham fell on his face and laughed and said to himself, "Shall a child be born to a man who is a hundred years old?" (Gen. 17:17)

WE'VE ALL HEARD how Abraham believed God and it was counted to him as righteousness (see Rom. 4:3, 9). He's referred to as the father of those of faith (see Rom. 4:12; Gal. 3:9), and he had great faith when he trekked up Mount Moriah to sacrifice Isaac. Hebrews 11 describes him this way: "By faith Abraham, when he was tested, offered up Isaac, and he who had received the promises was in the act of offering up his only son. . . . He considered that God was able even to raise him from the dead" (vv. 17, 19).

When asked to sacrifice the one on whom all the promises of God were fixed, Abraham thought, *God gave me this son; if he dies, God will raise him up.* Abraham seems like a man who never struggled with doubt, doesn't he?

Thankfully, the Bible never paints false portraits of God's children. Sure, there were times when Abraham's faith shone, but . . .

- Abraham doubted God's protection, so he told his wife to lie . . . twice (see Gen. 12:11–13; 20:2).
- Abraham doubted that God would give him a son, so he suggested that God use his servant instead (see Gen. 15:2–3).
- after believing the promise of a land as an inheritance, Abraham doubted and demanded a sign (see Gen. 15:8).
- Abraham gave in to Sarah's unbelief and fathered a son, Ishmael, by her servant (see Gen. 16). Again he tried to substitute Ishmael for the promised one (see Gen. 17:18).

- both Abraham and Sarah doubted God's word and laughed at his promise (see Gen. 17:17; 18:12).

While Abraham did have shining moments of certainty, most of the time he was trying to fight off doubt and unbelief. In fact, it wasn't until after the birth of Isaac that his faith grew strong. Both Abraham and Sarah seem to have had a much easier time walking by sight than by faith. Did they believe? Yes. Did they doubt? Yes. They were just like us. Doubt didn't disqualify them, and it won't disqualify you, either.

Think back over the story of Abraham and Sarah's life. If you're not familiar with it, take time to skim Genesis 12–20. Perhaps you've heard sermons about Abraham's great faith and you've surmised that there's something innately wrong with you because you can't picture yourself sacrificing to God like that. Don't worry. You're not alone. Even if God is asking a difficult obedience from you, he has also promised to be with you. Perhaps part of your doubting has to do with what you fear God *might* ask of you. Don't test the strength of your faith in imagined scenarios. If God calls you to a difficult time of sacrifice, he will strengthen you for it.

Make a list of the steps of faith that God is *actually* calling you to take today, and then pray for grace to begin to obey. What he wants from you today is simply a heart that says, *I'd like to believe and obey. Please help me.*

Truth 3: Every child of faith, even the "great" ones, had times of significant doubt.

Truth 4: It's foolish for us to compare the strength of our faith to the strength of others'.

DAY 3

The Meekest Doubter on the Earth

Now the man Moses was very meek, more than all people
who were on the face of the earth. (Num. 12:3)

I'M PART OF THE generation that first learned about Moses by watching Charlton Heston stand before the Red Sea with his staff in his outstretched arm, commanding the waters in great faith to part so that the Israelites could pass through. Who hasn't seen the epic 1956 movie *The Ten Commandments*?

That's generally how we think of Moses: bold, fiery, filled with faith, making demands before Pharaoh (the most powerful man on earth), commanding bread from heaven, leading the rebels through the wilderness. In addition to being a strong leader, he was also called the most humble, or meekest, man on the earth. That's quite a combination, isn't it? His faith was strong enough to enable him to lead millions of people through extremely difficult times, yet his strength didn't come from pride or narcissism. It came from humility and trust. Have we found someone with perfect faith? Let's take a closer look.

You remember the story: Pharaoh's daughter saved baby Moses out of the water and raised him in her household. Once he grew to manhood, he identified with the suffering Hebrew slaves and killed an Egyptian. He soon fled to the land of Midian, where he spent forty years tending flocks. Then, when he was eighty, he came face-to-face with God in a burning bush. After the Lord informed Moses of his identity, he said, "Come, I will send you to Pharaoh that you may bring my people . . . out of Egypt" (Ex. 3:10).

You would think that Moses, this great man of faith, would say, "Yes, sir, Lord! Sign me up!" But you know that that's not what happened. No fewer than five times, Moses doubted God's ability to use him to deliver his people. Five times he argued with a talking bush that burned but wasn't consumed. Sometimes doubt makes us silly. And even after Moses had gone back to Egypt, he asked questions like "Why did you ever send me?" multiple times (Ex. 5:22; see also 6:12, 30).

Let's fast-forward to the end of Moses's life. He'd led the Israelites through the wilderness for years. He'd put up with their complaining and unbelief. He'd given them God's law and built a portable church for them in the desert. Was Moses finally free from doubt now? No. Even after years of seeing God's miraculous provision, Moses still didn't fully believe. In a fit of unbelief and anger, he struck the water-giving rock instead of speaking to it. God diagnosed Moses's problem: he did not believe in him (see Num. 20:12). Even though he saw miracles, spoke with God face-to-face, and was called the friend of God (see Ex. 33:11), Moses still doubted.

Take a few moments now to review the passages above. What are you learning about the interplay between faith and doubt? Was Moses used by God even though his faith wasn't perfect? Yes, of course he was. What does that tell you about God's ability to use you even though you struggle? Have you noticed times in your life when your doubt bred anger or self-indulgence? Can you name them?

Truth 5: Sometimes doubt can make us respond foolishly.

Truth 6: Having more physical proof, like bread falling from heaven, won't erase our doubt.

DAY 4

Doubters in Exile

"Then I will go to the king, though it is against the law, and if I perish, I perish." (Est. 4:16)

"Our God whom we serve is able to deliver us from the burning fiery furnace, and he will deliver us out of your hand, O king. But if not . . . " (Dan. 3:17–18)

AFTER CENTURIES OF warning them to turn from idolatry, God finally gave Israel and Judah into the hands of their enemies, the Persians and Babylonians. This was the distressing situation that Esther, Shadrach, Meshach, and Abednego faced every day. Every morning when they woke up and saw their surroundings, they remembered that this punishment was not just a bad dream. They were slaves in a foreign land. They had lost everything. They had no hope that anything would change.

When King Ahasuerus desired a new wife, Esther's guardian, Mordecai, let her be taken into the king's harem rather than hiding her or helping her escape. Eventually she became queen, and, at a time of great need, she used her influence to save her nation.

Even though Esther is known for her courage, she had to be pressured to act for her people. Mordecai warned her, "If you keep silent at this time . . . you and your father's house will perish" (Est. 4:14). She was motivated by fear and threat into risking her life. Though God used her to save his people, she didn't have complete certitude. Trembling, she stood.

Three friends—Shadrach, Meshach, and Abednego— courageously faced the outrage of the all-powerful king Nebuchadnezzar, who had demanded that they worship an idol he had created in his image. The punishment for refusing to comply was being burned alive. Remembering the reason for their exile, they stood against the king and faced a hideous death.

You may think, *Surely here is an example of great faith!* And you'd be right—but consider again what they said. "We don't know whether God will help us or not. But, even so, we'll obey." Do you hear the lack of certainty in their voices? They knew that they had to obey, but they didn't know whether God would deliver them. This is faith. Faith doesn't say, "I know that everything will work out the way I hope it does." Rather, it says, "I don't know how God might choose to work—maybe he'll deliver me; maybe not. But, if he doesn't, I'm willing to die."

Esther and the three Hebrew exiles are examples of people of faith who were willing to lay it all on the line for God. Through the work of the Spirit, they "obtained promises" and "quenched the power of fire"; but they were also "made *strong out of weakness*" (Heb. 11:33–34). They weren't inherently strong. They had to grow in faith. And so do we all. Faith doesn't mean that we don't have any questions. It means that we face them and trust the Lord to make us strong as we strive to obey.

Review the stories of Esther (Est. 3–7) and the exiles (Dan. 3). Although they lived in a different context, they are probably like you in many ways. Can you think of any? How does their questioning God's plans for them encourage you today? Have you ever questioned God's plan and obeyed anyway? How did that work out for you?

> **Truth 7:** Even doubters can stand in faith courageously.
>
> **Truth 8:** Faith doesn't demand complete certitude, even in the face of death.

DAY 5

Behold the Lamb of God . . . I Think

The next day he saw Jesus coming toward him, and said, "Behold, the Lamb of God, who takes away the sin of the world!" (John 1:29)

"Are you the one who is to come, or shall we look for another?" (Matt. 11:3)

AT TIMES, CIRCUMSTANCES seem to conspire to drain our faith. Perhaps you started your Christian walk with a strong faith but have faced difficulties and setbacks, and now you're wondering whether any of it is true. Perhaps you've believed a false promise of success. Or maybe a Christian relative or friend has shown himself to be unreliable, and you're wondering what else you've been deceived about. Maybe you've been told that if you just had enough faith, you'd be healed—and, though you've prayed, the pain wears on. Or perhaps you have started to doubt and aren't sure why. One thing is for sure: certainty in faith isn't consistent for anyone. Not even for the greatest prophet of the Bible.

From before his conception, Jesus's older cousin, John, had been called to faith. The Holy Spirit witnessed to him *in utero* that he was in the presence of the Messiah. As he grew into a man, he knew his prophetic message: He was to prepare God's people for the Messiah by calling them back to a life of holiness. He was to witness to the identity of the Christ. "Behold, the Lamb of God, who takes away the sin of the world! . . . For this purpose I came . . . that he might be revealed to Israel. . . . I saw the Spirit descend from heaven like a dove, and it remained on him. . . . And I have seen and have borne witness *that this is the Son of God*" (John 1:29, 31–33, 34).

John sounds very sure, doesn't he? But Jesus's ministry

surprised him. Instead of cleaning up the riffraff by thundering a message of the law at them, Jesus welcomed them. He ate with them. He befriended immoral women. It was not only confusing, it was scandalous! And then John was tossed in prison. Had he been wrong about the identity of the Christ? So he sent word to Jesus to ask, "Are you the One . . . or have I been wrong?"

Jesus didn't respond to John by shaming him. Instead, he reminded him of the Messiah's true call—a call to preach good news to the spiritually poor. And then Jesus bragged about John: "Among those born of women there has arisen no one greater than John the Baptist" (Matt. 11:11). Jesus boasted about John even though John doubted him.

As you think about your doubt, are you able to pinpoint specific teachings or events that have attacked or weakened your faith? What have you believed that has proven false? Whom have you trusted who has proven untrustworthy? Ask the Lord to grant you grace to see how these circumstances have fed your doubt, and ask him to help you to understand and rebuild your faith again. Spend time thanking God that he doesn't shame doubters but rather gives them evidence to believe.

Truth 9: Certainty in faith isn't consistent. Everyone questions truth that they were once assured of.

Truth 10: Jesus boasted about John even when John doubted him. He doesn't shame doubters; he gives them evidence to rebuild their faith.

PROOF FOR
YOUR FAITH

DAY 6

Is God There?

For his invisible attributes, namely, his eternal power and divine nature, have been clearly perceived, ever since the creation of the world, in the things that have been made. (Rom. 1:20)

EVERYONE LOVES WATCHING entertainers perform baffling feats of magic. You've seen them: The magician places his lovely assistant in a box suspended off the floor, waves his magic wand, and *poof!* She disappears. And then, of course, what follows next is her materializing out of thin air. *Ta-da!* It's magic!

We love trying to figure out how the magician does his tricks. We know that he's tricking us, because no one can actually make someone disappear or reappear. No one can create something out of nothing. That's why magicians fascinate us. It looks like they're doing the impossible, so we continue to watch, even though every grown-up knows that we're seeing only sleight of hand.

Paul employed this kind of logic when writing to the church in Rome. He asserted that the invisible attributes of God—his power and nature—are apparent every time you see *something* rather than *nothing*. The mere fact that we both live in this world, and that I've written words that you're reading, shouts to us that someone must have brought everything into existence. Paul said that the things that are visible testify about an invisible reality. From the things that we see, we know there is something we can't see.

Dear doubter, my goal here is not to prove to you that the God of the Bible is *the* God who created all things. I'm simply saying that everyone knows that no one can make something come from nothing. Even if you doubt the veracity of a six-day creation, the question behind all the theories—whether the big bang or spaceships dropping off the seeds of planets—is, Why was there something there that could go "bang"? Why were there spaceships and seeds instead of nothing? Or, more succinctly, *why did it all originate*? What follows closely from that question is this statement: *Everything has a beginning.* Even if you want to believe that something went "bang" four billion or forty billion years ago, the questions still remain.

We know that nothing appears *ex nihilo*, or out of nothing. And, as we look at the beauty and complexity of everything from the spirals in human DNA to the spirals that are evident throughout the universe, we are forced to admit that there is an intelligent designer behind all things—and that this designer has to be, as Paul wrote, both powerful and divine.

It seems reasonable, especially in these days, to doubt the creation story as presented in Genesis. If you are troubled about the fact that it seems far-fetched, don't be. What you need to believe right now is what you already believe: that there is something rather than nothing, that there is Someone behind all that we see, and that all that we see was once not seen.

Truth 11: Logic and observation teach that all things come from other things and that all things have a beginning.

Truth 12: There is an intelligent designer behind everything that was made, and we know him as Jesus Christ.

DAY 7

The Reliable Word

Forever, O LORD, your word is firmly fixed in the heavens. (Ps. 119:89)

THE BIBLE IS GOD'S WORD. I'm sure you have heard that before. Perhaps you've wondered about it. Is there a way we can know that the Bible is the Word of God? Just because a document is ancient, and many have believed in it, doesn't mean it's *God's Word*.

The Bible isn't bashful at all about declaring itself to be the very Word of God. Nearly four thousand times it says that it is speaking for God, using phrases like "God said" or "Thus says the Lord."[1] Think about that. Across thousands of years, the forty[2] writers of Scripture knew that they were writing for God.

Moses knew that he was writing the very script the intelligent designer was revealing to him. His history begins, "In the beginning, God created the heavens and the earth. . . . And God said . . ." (Gen. 1:1, 3). Moses believed that he was reporting facts about the beginning of all things and the One who spoke behind it all.

We must ask ourselves, does the Bible give us reason to believe or to doubt?

One of the ways we can know that the Bible is God's Word is because it is filled with prophecies that have come true. Of the approximately 2,500 prophecies in the Bible, about two-thirds have already been fulfilled. Some of the prophecies are so specific that anyone with a reasonably open mind would be convinced that the Bible is uniquely inspired. Here are just two examples:

- Isaiah prophesied about a man named Cyrus, who would conquer the Babylonian empire and let the Jewish exiles go. This prophecy was uttered *150 years* before Cyrus was

29

even born and *80 years* before the Jews were even taken into exile (see Isa. 44:28; 45:1, 13). That Cyrus lived and accomplished all this is a fact proven by archaeology.[3] The probability of this being just a chance fulfillment is 1 in 10^{15}, That's one chance in 10,000,000,000,000,000. Do you have reason to doubt with those odds?

- The Old Testament foretold that the ancient Jewish nation would be conquered twice and that the people would be carried off as slaves each time, first by the Babylonians (for a period of seventy years) and then by another kingdom (see Deut. 29; Isa. 11:11–13; Jer. 25:11; Hos. 3:4–5; Luke 21:23–24). These prophecies were fulfilled exactly. The probability of this being a chance fulfillment is 1 in 10^{20}.[4]

If your doubt has roots in the reliability of the Bible, there are online resources that you can easily access. I've included a number of these websites in the endnotes.[5] Why not take time now to visit a few of them?

Truth 13: The Bible makes claims about itself that set it apart from all other ancient books.

Truth 14: There is enough evidence in the Bible's fulfilled prophecies to move someone from doubt to reasonable belief.

DAY 8

All This Took Place to Fulfill

All this took place to fulfill what the Lord had spoken by the prophet: "Behold, the virgin shall conceive and bear a son, and they shall call his name Immanuel." (Matt. 1:22–23)

JESUS MADE SOME pretty amazing claims. He claimed to be the unique Son of God (see John 5:18), meaning that he was equal with God. He said that he was the one who, as God, revealed himself to Moses in the burning bush (see Ex. 3:14; John 8:57–59). He claimed that he and God the Father were one (see John 10:30–33). He also claimed to be the Messiah and the Christ, and he did so knowing that those words would seal his execution (see Mark 14:61–64). Jesus never claimed to be simply a good moral teacher. He claimed to be God. And it was that claim that ultimately sent him to a Roman cross.

There are a number of ways to consider Jesus's claims. Perhaps he was insane. However, if you consider his life and the lives of the people who have followed him, does this conclusion seem reasonable? Would a person who is so unhinged from reality love as he did?

Or perhaps he was a charlatan, trying to dupe the masses for personal gain. If you want to think that, you have to ask yourself whether he gained wealth or power from his ministry. You know that he didn't. So, as you consider the claims of himself and others about how he perfectly fulfilled Scripture, can you be convinced into reasonable belief?

Today we are going to consider the importance of the prophecies that predicted what the life and ministry of the true Messiah would be like.

What should we say in response to anyone's claim to be God?

Is Jesus actually speaking the truth? We are invited to say, "Prove it!" And that is just what the four gospel writers, Matthew, Mark, Luke, and John, did. They painstakingly recorded the ways in which Jesus was the long-awaited Messiah who fulfilled prophecy.

For example, 750 years before his birth, the prophet Micah said that the Messiah would be born in Bethlehem (see Mic. 5:2). Around the same time, Isaiah said that he would be born of a virgin (see Isa. 7:14). Hosea prophesied that he would spend time in Egypt (see Hos. 11:1), while Jeremiah predicted that children would be massacred at the time of his birth (see Jer. 31:15). Each of these prophecies (and many more) were perfectly fulfilled. The odds of this happening by chance are astronomical.[1]

Imagine that you're on a jury trying to decide the fate of a son who claimed a certain ancestry. If he produced documents written by people who were at his birth, knew his family, and had DNA evidence, you would probably find in favor of him. Even though utter certainty would be nearly impossible, if you didn't have a good reason to reject the testimony of those witnesses, you would put doubt aside. That's where you are today.

Ask the Lord to help you stop trying to obtain complete certainty and to enable you to study the evidence and believe. In the endnotes, I've included websites where you can obtain more evidence.

> **Truth 15:** Jesus claimed to be God. We know enough about his life to know that he wasn't crazy or a liar.
>
> **Truth 16:** Jesus fulfilled a number of specific prophecies over which he had no control.

DAY 9

Down to the Most Gruesome Detail

But the tunic was seamless, woven in one piece from top to bottom, so they said to one another, "Let us not tear it, but cast lots for it to see whose it shall be." This was to fulfill the Scripture which says, "They divided my garments among them, and for my clothing they cast lots." (John 19:23–24)

TODAY WE'LL CONCLUDE this section about how Jesus's ful-fillment of biblical prophecies is meant to give us a high level of confidence in him. Some of the most astonishingly detailed pre-dictions about Jesus have to do with the events surrounding his death—events that, humanly speaking, he had no control over.

Remember that, when someone makes outlandish claims, it's perfectly acceptable for us to respond with a skeptical "Prove it!" We aren't asked to make a blind leap of faith, as some suggest. Rather, we are encouraged to investigate and see whether belief is reasonable.

Of course, a skeptic may say that Jesus knew the prophecies beforehand and made sure to fulfill them. That's an understand-able response, and it might even account for some of them, but he had no control over the events and even manner of his death. As you will see, during the fulfillment of some of the prophecies, he was nailed to a cross and was unable to control anything.

The very manner of his death was predicted at a time when crucifixion was unknown to the Jews. The prophet Zechariah foretold that the people would "look . . . on him whom they have pierced" (Zech. 12:10). Isaiah said that the Suffering Servant would be "pierced for our transgressions" (Isa. 53:5). The form of punishment that the Messiah was to face had already been determined hundreds of years before Rome took over Israel and developed her cruel methods of execution.

Even the clothes that he put on the morning before his death were also predicted. And, while that might have been something that he could manipulate, he certainly couldn't make his Roman executioners gamble for his clothing or refuse to cut up his robe (see Ps. 22:18).

Another prophecy predicted that at his death none of his bones would be broken (see Ps. 34:20). Because most of us are not familiar with the practice of execution in ancient Israel—death by stoning—we aren't shocked at this prophecy. People who were publicly executed in Israel by stoning had numerous bones broken. When Jesus was crucified, he died before the Roman guards had to break his legs.

From his first breath in Bethlehem until his cry of "Father, into your hands I commit my spirit!" (Luke 23:46; cf. Ps. 31:5), Jesus was offering to you and me all the proof we need in order to cast off doubt and believe. That anyone would be able to fulfill all the prophecies in the Bible simply by chance is completely ludicrous. If you have a computer available, do an internet search of the eight prophecies that Christ fulfilled at his death. Once you've completed that, ask the Lord to help you believe.

Truth 17: While Jesus might have tried for some unknown reason to fool people by fulfilling prophecies, he couldn't have done so from the cross.

Truth 18: It would take more faith to believe that Jesus's claims to be God are just a hoax than to simply believe those claims.

DAY 10

Not a Clever Myth

We did not follow cleverly devised myths when we made known to you the power and coming of our Lord Jesus Christ. (2 Peter 1:16)

CONTRARY TO POPULAR OPINION, the thought of physical resurrection from the dead was unheard of in the Ancient Near East. Although people were superstitious (though not more so than we are today), early Greek philosophy had so influenced the culture that the thought of reanimating a body once dead was disgusting. And certainly none of the disciples had any inkling that Jesus's death on Golgotha wasn't the end of their story. We know this because the gospel writers candidly recorded how they didn't believe the report of the empty tomb. Rather than trying to pull off an elaborate hoax, those cowards were hiding and hoping that the officials would just forget about them. Waiting by his tomb for his reappearance? It was laughable!

For those of us who struggle with doubt, the resurrection serves as the cardinal truth-claim of our faith. In essence, Jesus's resurrection from the dead proves that what he said about who he was and what he had come to do was true. As Peter wrote, "We did not follow cleverly devised myths when we made known to you the power and coming of our Lord Jesus Christ" (2 Peter 1:16). The once cowardly Peter—who, filled with doubt, denied ever knowing "the man" (Matt. 26:72)—died a gruesome death as a martyr for this message. No one would die in order to prove a falsehood. Peter knew that Jesus was the Christ, and he was willing to die for that truth.

Jesus said many things that, apart from the resurrection, seem ridiculous. The statement that he was going to die as a ransom for sinners (see Matt. 20:28) would be preposterous if he hadn't arisen from the grave. In other words, if someone proposes some sort of truth to you, dies for it, and then rises again, it's reasonable to assume that he's telling the truth.

So what are the truths that the resurrection teaches us? First of all, we learn that Jesus is who he said he is: God the Son. That's important for us to know because, as God, he has the power to accomplish anything that he deems beneficial and right. Jesus is God. We can trust him. It's also important to know because it means that the work he set out to do in order "to seek and to save the lost" (Luke 19:10) has been accomplished. Did you—do you—feel lost? Then Jesus has promised to seek and to save you. You can trust him. He said, "It is finished!"—and it is.

Another truth the resurrection teaches us is that Jesus is presently physically alive, ruling and caring for us in his human (though glorified) body. If he were dead, or perhaps just a spirit somewhere, it would be difficult to trust that he is still watching over and pardoning, protecting, and providing for us. But because he is our incarnate Brother, we can be at peace. If it were even possible for you to slip from Jesus's mind, all he would have to do is to look down at his own nail-scarred human hands and he would remember you.

Although most Christians celebrate Easter, many don't realize what Jesus's resurrection has accomplished for us. Yes, he is alive, and his life means everything. What does his ongoing life mean to you and your tentative faith?

Truth 19: The disciples wouldn't have concocted a resurrection story. They were too busy hiding.

Truth 20: The resurrection isn't a myth. It means that all that Jesus said and did and all that he set out to accomplish is true and reliable.

SINNERS WHO BELIEVE

DAY 11

Just Believe

"Sirs, what must I do to be saved?" And they said, "Believe in the Lord Jesus, and you will be saved." (Acts 16:30–31)

"WHAT MUST I DO TO BE SAVED?" Good question. It has been asked on thousands of occasions in thousands of contexts. If it's being asked in light of eternal salvation, it's the most important question one can ask. To the question "What must I *do?*" the worst answer seems to be "Nothing. Just believe." Everything in us revolts against that kind of answer. We would feel so much more secure and confident if we were given something concrete to do, even if it were difficult. If the answers were "Crawl on your knees until they bleed" or "Say this prayer 750 times," that would be better than "Believe." In part, that's because believing can't be measured like bloody knees or prayer beads can. "Believe" forces us to look away from ourselves and to trust someone else. It's not only scary, it's insulting. "You're saying that I can't add anything to my salvation?"

This reminds me of the story of Naaman, a Syrian commander whom we read about in 2 Kings 5. Naaman was a powerful yet terribly weak man. Though he commanded armies, he couldn't control his own skin. He was a leper. Through his wife's Israelite slave, he heard that he could be healed if he went to Israel. So he took ten thousand talents of silver, six thousand shekels of gold, and ten changes of clothing in order to buy his healing.

When Elisha heard that Naaman had come for healing, he sent him this message: "Go and wash in the Jordan seven times, and your flesh shall be restored, and you shall be clean" (v. 10). Rather than rejoicing in the ease of this promise, Naaman was enraged. He was humiliated. Naaman wanted something that he could put his trust in, like religious ceremony. Elisha wouldn't even come out to speak to him or wave his hand over his leprosy while he prayed. Naaman wanted to pay someone for his healing. Fortunately, another servant spoke sense to him. "So he went down and dipped himself seven times in the Jordan . . . and his flesh was restored . . . and he was clean" (v. 14).

It's easy to look at this story and judge Naaman. He was proud. He believed that everything had to be bought and paid for. He didn't trust grace. He thought that he deserved respect. He wasn't afraid of a little work or a little religious magic. What infuriated him was that there was very little for him to do. Just go take a mud bath—that's it! The amazing part of this story is that Naaman received healing after all.

It would be so much easier to feel confident if there were something we could look at to assure ourselves that we have done the necessary work. But the very ease of the command "Believe!" is what's hard. "Really, is that all I need to do?" "How can I measure whether I'm believing enough?"

Read 2 Kings 5. In what ways are you like Naaman? Are there specific signs or events that you desire so as to be assured of your faith? Do you believe that God is able to grant you the faith that you need when you ask? What would stop him? What do you think grace is? Will you trust God?

Truth 21: One reason that you struggle with doubt may be the ease of the command "Believe."

Truth 22: Even though the command to believe appears too easy, the truth is that it is too hard. Only God can grant you saving faith.

DAY 12

My Sin Is Ever Before Me

For I know my transgressions, and my sin is ever before me. (Ps. 51:3)

IN THE SPRINGTIME, when most kings went "out to battle" (2 Sam. 11:1), King David decided to stay home. The Bible doesn't tell us what motivated him to choose to do so; it simply says that he did. It's obvious, though, that he didn't stay home to work. We can also be sure that he didn't stay home to pray for his troops. Maybe he just felt that ennui that sometimes accompanies busy lives. Or maybe he thought he had worked hard enough for long enough and needed a little R&R. Or maybe he craved a little spice in his life. We don't know why David stayed home, but we do know what he did next. "It happened, late one afternoon, when David arose from his couch and was walking on the roof of the king's house, that he saw from the roof a woman bathing; and the woman was very beautiful. . . . So David sent messengers and took her" (vv. 2, 4).

While his army was out conquering, David was abusing his power to make another sort of conquest. He seized another man's wife. I've often heard this episode described as an "affair" or as "adultery," as though Bathsheba were a temptress who was all too happy to jump in bed with the king. But the Bible doesn't portray this episode that way. In truth, Bathsheba was on her roof, in privacy, fulfilling her religious obligation to purify herself after her menstrual period. This wasn't a love affair. This was King David stealing another man's wife. You know how this episode ends. When Bathsheba conceived, David ordered the death of her husband, who was his own loyal subject. That Bathsheba loved Uriah her husband is obvious from the way she grieved: "When *the wife* of Uriah heard that Uriah *her husband* was dead, *she lamented over her husband*" (v. 26).

King David abused his power and his God-given position. He killed an honorable man and dishonored an honorable woman. He destroyed their marriage. This was no accidental indiscretion. This was premeditated coercion, abuse of power, and murder. And "the thing that David had done displeased the LORD" (v. 27).

If you or I were writing this story, we might doubt that there would ever be forgiveness or mercy for David. He certainly didn't deserve it. If karma had been at work, David would have died a hideous death at the hands of a domineering monarch. But that's not how this story ends. It ends with David confessing his sin and being assured of God's forgiveness. To David's anguished confession, "I have sinned against the LORD," we hear Nathan's assurance: "The LORD also has put away your sin; you shall not die" (2 Sam. 12:13). Even though there were horizontal consequences from his sin, David knew God's pledge of love, mercy, and forgiveness.

Read David's cry of repentance recorded in Psalm 51. What words does he use to describe his sin? Does he think he deserves forgiveness? What is he afraid of? What doubts does he have? What hopes? As you think about your sins and wonder if it is possible for God to have mercy on you, how does this psalm encourage you?

Truth 23: God's mercy extends even to the most terrible sinners who are sorry for their sin.

Truth 24: Your sin might be "ever before you" in your own eyes, but it isn't in God's.

DAY 13

In Paradise Today

"Truly, I say to you, today you will be with me in paradise." (Luke 23:43)

IF EVER A man was justified in having doubts about his future, it was the thief in Luke 23. He had squandered whatever life he had been given. Perhaps he'd been poor and destitute, or maybe he'd just loved the thrill of criminal activity. But he had been caught. With his dying breath, he confessed that he was "receiving the due reward of [his] deeds" (v. 41). For whatever reason, and through whatever circuitous path, he found himself nailed to a Roman cross, next to a Man he'd heard rumors about but had probably never met.

What did this condemned criminal know about the Christ who was crucified next to him? He knew that he was an innocent man. Did he know that he was God or was the Messiah? Perhaps. Luke is the only one of the four gospel writers who mentions his interaction with Jesus. Perhaps only the women weeping at Jesus's feet overheard it, and since Luke wrote from their recollections, he's the only one who recorded it. In any case, their dialog is short. Breath was at a premium for them both. Legs were about to be broken.

Their short exchange answers the most pressing question we can ask: what do we need to do in order to be saved?

The plea: "Jesus, remember me when you come into your kingdom."
The answer: "Truly, I say to you, today you will be with me in Paradise."

To what kingdom was this criminal referring? Was he hoping that Jesus would finally claim an earthly kingdom and banish

43

the Romans and their brutality? Or was he thinking of a heavenly kingdom? Again, we don't know. But Jesus did. Was this thief repentant for his sins? It seems so, because he knew he was a criminal who deserved punishment. In any case, he had some sort of faith, evidenced by the fact that he asked Jesus to remember him.

Why am I reminding you about this nameless criminal? Because doubts about our salvation frequently grow in soil that's been sown with instructions on what a perfect prayer of faith and correct contrition look like. I've talked with people who have been told that they're probably not saved because they did or did not pray "the sinner's prayer" or because they can't remember the exact date of their conversion. Still others have been told that, because they're not accomplishing great things or growing in specific and clearly identifiable ways all the time, they should question their salvation. If this story of the dying thief tells us anything, it's that Jesus sees the longing of the broken heart and has no formulaic demands for salvation.

Reflect on the thief's brief words, "Remember me," along with the first words of faith that you spoke to the Lord. Does the fact that his brief prayer was enough for Jesus encourage or discourage you? What does the fact that he couldn't accomplish great things for God say to you?

Truth 25: Jesus, not the correctness of their prayer or the zeal of their service, saves sinners.

Truth 26: No matter how long you've waited or how much time you've wasted, Jesus loves enough to forgive and rescue.

DAY 14

The Fearful Shepherd

"I do not know the man." (Matt. 26:72)

How awful would it be to have your worst failure broadcast around the world on social media? In 2013, a woman made an unwise quip about AIDS on Twitter, thinking that only her few followers would see it. When her tweet went viral, her life as she knew it came to an end.[1] We live in a peculiar and frightening time of instantaneous public shaming. But even if we didn't, even if our misdeeds could only be announced to our little neighborhood or village, wouldn't that be bad enough?

Today we're going to think about someone who was once referred to as a rock, a man whose understanding of Christ's mission was a sign of his blessedness, a man who, though he was impetuous, was certainly not weak. Of course you know we're talking about the apostle Peter. All four of the gospel writers recorded his painful fall into disgrace.

Having your misdeed inscripturated is far worse than having a tweet or a Facebook post go awry. That's because the Bible is far and away the most published book in the history of the world. More than five billion copies have been sold worldwide, and even more people have heard its stories. How's that for public shaming on a biblical scale?

It's very easy to assume that our confidence would grow if we were able to look at the record of our good deeds and strong confessions. If I can just see a clear record of my growth, I'll know that God approves of me—right? But what if you couldn't even stand to look at yourself in the mirror, knowing not only that *everyone* knows about your duplicity and cowardice, but also that you'd deserted your best friend at the moment of his deepest need?

How do you breathe after that? How do you go on in faith? How do you not doubt?

Peter knew that Jesus knew what he had done. Luke tells us that, after Peter's denials, Jesus himself walked by and "looked at Peter" (Luke 22:61). That look must have been seared into Peter's memory for the rest of his life. He went out and "wept bitterly" (v. 62).

The next time we see Peter, he's hiding out with the rest of the disciples. He hears word that Jesus has arisen, so he runs to the empty tomb. Later on, Jesus makes breakfast for his friends on the beach and brings Peter close again. "Do you love me?" he asks three times. "Lord . . . you know . . . " Peter finally answers. Then, shockingly, Jesus commissions him to shepherd his flock (see John 21:15–19). What kind of shepherd would Peter be? How could he lead anyone? Jesus knew that Peter was the perfectly imperfect man to lead his church of doubting sheep, and he knew that all of us doubters needed to hear Peter's story.

Peter doubted that God could protect him on the night of Christ's betrayal. And, many years later, he even doubted that God would protect him from the scorn of the Judaizers (see Gal. 2:11–13). Jesus didn't need Peter's great faith or great deeds. He needed a man just like you and me—flawed and doubting, yet wanting to stand and believe.

Truth 27: Doubt doesn't disqualify you from serving God's people.

Truth 28: God uses people who have both times of faith and times of doubt. People are qualified to lead God's people by Jesus, not by the strength of their faith.

DAY 15

Now No Condemnation

There is therefore now no condemnation for those
who are in Christ Jesus. (Rom. 8:1)

HANGING OVER US is the awareness that we're not the sort of people we should be. Not only do we not live up to the demands of God's holy law, we even fail to live up to our own standards. We all know that if the world were just, our failures would demand punishment. So, while we don't hope that the world is unjust, we also hope that justice isn't visited on us.

This isn't something that only doubters struggle with. It's common to us all. That's because the law is written in our hearts. Our consciences prove our guiltiness, and our thoughts either accuse or vainly try to excuse us (see Rom. 2:4–15). In other words, within our heart is a prosecuting attorney who is consistently presenting evidence of our guilt. We have all failed to love even those who we say we love or to do the things we have promised to do. We deserve punishment. And what is the punishment we deserve? Condemnation.

Is there any help for us? That was, in fact, Paul's question at the end of Romans 7. After describing his personal failures and his inability to do what he knew he should and even wanted to do, he cried out in desperation, "Wretched man that I am! Who will deliver me from this body of death?" (v. 24) What was his answer? "Thanks be to God through Jesus Christ our Lord!" (v. 25). Only Jesus Christ, not Paul's perfect law keeping, would free him from his death sentence.

But did his deliverance mean that he would be able to live a sinless life from then on? No—for he recognized that even though he longed to obey the law, his flesh would continue to fight him. He would continue to fail, but his failure wouldn't produce judgment; for right on the heels of his confession of inability to consistently obey, he thundered, "There is therefore now no condemnation for those who are in Christ Jesus" (Rom. 8:1)!

The only way for us to be assured of our salvation is to believe that the condemnation we justly deserve was meted out to Jesus Christ in our place. He was condemned for us. Because he has so identified with us, we are now counted innocent. We are free. But we are not simply set free; our debt to God has been paid in full.

If you find it difficult to believe that God's punishment isn't awaiting you, you're not alone. I believe that Jesus lived a perfectly obedient life in my place, suffered a shameful and excruciating death in my place, and was raised on the third day by the Father, who vindicated him as being the beloved Son in my place . . . and yet I still wonder. This news can seem too good to be true. Dear reader, you are not alone in your doubts.

Take time now to read Romans 7 and 8. What do you learn about Paul's struggle for assurance? What do you learn about yourself? Spend time in prayer asking the Spirit to help you believe, and then refuse to look at your own life for assurance.

Truth 29: Not even the great apostle Paul lived a life worthy of salvation.

Truth 30: Freedom from condemnation is not primarily a feeling. It's a verdict that has been pronounced from outside you.

DAY 16

Doubting Disciples

"Unless I see . . . I will never believe." (John 20:25)

IF THERE IS anyone whose name is synonymous with doubt, it has to be Thomas. But it is not as though Thomas were the only doubter in the Bible. As a matter of fact, none of the disciples believed the report about the empty tomb. Perhaps we should refer to them as the *Doubting Disciples!* Thomas is remembered for his doubt, but that isn't all that we know about him.

The gospel writers first mention Thomas while listing the disciples (see Matt. 10:3; Mark 3:18; Luke 6:15). The next time we hear about him, he is bravely proposing that he and the rest of the disciples accompany Jesus back to Judea, even though it's likely they will be killed. "Thomas, called the Twin, said to his fellow disciples, 'Let us also go, that we may die with him'" (John 11:16). Thomas was willing to put his life on the line for the Messiah.

The next time we hear from him, Thomas is asking a reasonable question in response to Jesus's announcement that he would be going away: "Lord, we do not know where you are going. How can we know the way?" to which Jesus replies, "I am the way, and the truth, and the life. No one comes to the Father except through me. If you had known me, you would have known my Father also. From now on you do know him and have seen him" (John 14:5–7). Thomas wasn't afraid to question the Lord when he didn't understand, and Jesus assured him in response. *You know him . . . and have seen him.*

Then, famously, because Thomas was absent from the disciples when Jesus appeared to them after the resurrection, he doubted their story. Perhaps he was too heartbroken to allow himself to believe again. Hadn't he done that once? And look how that ended. I don't think that he doubted because he didn't love Jesus. I think that he doubted because he did. *I won't let myself hope again . . . I've loved him. Now he's gone. I have to face it and get on with my life.*

What I want you to see, however, is Jesus's response: He didn't scold or shame Thomas. He didn't write him off as someone unworthy of the name *disciple*. No—instead, he offered him proof; he gave him what he needed. "Put your finger here, and see my hands; and put out your hand, and place it in my side. Do not disbelieve, but believe" (John 20:27). Thomas needed help in order to believe, and our loving, faithful Savior gave it to him. He had believed once and feared he'd been conned. So Jesus spoke, and what was Thomas's response? "My Lord and my God!" (John 20:28).[1]

Thomas was a confident, courageous disciple. He was willing to die with the Lord. He wasn't bashful about asking for clarification when he didn't understand what Jesus said. But something happened to Thomas. Jesus died . . . and then Thomas wasn't so sure. Perhaps you have gone through something similar. Perhaps something or someone has died. Perhaps everything you have worked for, all your prayers, seem unanswered. Don't despair. Ask Jesus now for the help that you need, and he'll give it. He'll enable you to say, "My Lord and my God" again.

Truth 31: The story of "doubting Thomas" is actually the story of a reassuring Jesus.

Truth 32: Jesus continues to be willing (and able) to answer all your questions.

DAY 17

A Chosen Instrument

The saying is trustworthy and deserving of full acceptance,
that Christ Jesus came into the world to save sinners,
of whom I am the foremost. (1 Tim. 1:15)

I'm sure there have been times when you have questioned God's love for you. Maybe you just can't seem to get past the fact that you committed *that* sin in the past, and you think it is just too much to believe that his promises are for someone like you. It's easy to think that God loves to forgive moral people for little indiscretions. But what about people who come into the church with a legacy of death and destruction trailing behind them? What about those who have been raised in a Christian home but snubbed their parents for years? What about women who have had abortions or men who have paid for them? It's almost too much to believe that God's mercy is *that* extravagant. God would be justified in slamming the door in their faces, right? If your heart resonates with those dark thoughts, then I have good news for you today.

As the apostle Paul neared the end of his life, it would have been easy for him to have the same doubts. Sure, to the religious elite of his day, Paul had looked like one of the good guys. He was "circumcised on the eighth day, of the people of Israel, of the tribe of Benjamin, a Hebrew of Hebrews; as to the law, a Pharisee; as to zeal, a persecutor of the church; as to righteousness under the law, blameless" (Phil. 3:5–6).

But strict religious devotion wasn't Paul's only claim to fame. He also had a terrifying reputation. After approving of the stoning of Stephen (see Acts 8:1), he was "ravaging the church" (Acts 8:3). He breathed "threats and murder against the disciples of the

Lord" (Acts 9:1). In fact, he was traveling to Damascus so that "if he found any belonging to the Way, men or women, he might bring them bound to Jerusalem" (Acts 9:2) when he met the grace and forgiveness of Jesus.

If there was ever anyone who didn't deserve to be forgiven, welcomed, and called into God's service, it was Paul. But listen to Jesus's words: "He is a chosen instrument of mine" (Acts 9:15). How can a murderer be a chosen instrument of the very One whose children he was killing? Paul writes, "I was made a minister according to the gift of God's grace. . . . To me, though I am the very least of all the saints, this grace was given" (Eph. 3:7–8). Paul recognized that he was "the least of the apostles, unworthy to be called an apostle," because he "persecuted the church of God. But by the grace of God I am what I am" (1 Cor. 15:9–10).

There are fortunate Christians who come to faith without ever having ingested the muck of the world. But the apostle Paul wasn't one of them. When he looked back on his former life, he declared that he was the "foremost of sinners" (see 1 Tim. 1:15). God's promise to you is that no sin is beyond the reach of his forgiveness. You can rest in faith in his grace. If he could use murdering, abusing, blaspheming Paul, he can forgive and use you. Do you believe that Jesus can love even you? Tell him your doubts and ask for faith now.

Truth 33: The apostle Paul abused and murdered Christians, and yet Jesus forgave and used him.

Truth 34: Sometimes the failure you are most ashamed of is the very thing that the Lord will use to prove his great mercy.

THE CONFIDENCE
OF FAITH

DAY 18

Faith That Moves Mountains

"For truly, I say to you, if you have faith like a grain of a mustard seed, you will say to this mountain, 'Move from here to there,' and it will move, and nothing will be impossible for you." (Matt. 17:20)

HAVE YOU EVER commanded a mountain to move and actually had it move? I haven't. Of course, some people say that they speak miraculous things into existence, and I'll believe them when I see them move even a grain of sand with their words. I think we've missed the point of this whole passage.

Jesus doesn't want us to reposition hills with our words. The point of this passage is that none of us is able to. Consider what Jesus is saying again: How much faith does he say we need in order to move mountains? Teeny, tiny, little specks of faith. His point is that none of us has mountain-moving faith. Why? Because, as he says, we "doubt" (Matt. 21:21). And why do we doubt? Because we are weak and can't even believe without his intervention.

On our own, without the direct intervention of the Holy Spirit, none of us would have any faith at all. Left to ourselves, we can't muster up faith even as small as a mustard seed. That's not to say that Christians don't have any faith at all. It's just that it's been given to us as a gift, and it's not ever that strong. The apostle Paul wrote, "For by grace you have been saved through faith. And this is not your own doing; it is the gift of God, not a result of works, so that no one may boast" (Eph. 2:8–9).

What is the "gift of God" that Paul is referring to here? It is both saving faith and what saving faith accomplishes: our salvation. All of it is a gift. None of us would believe anything necessary for salvation if God didn't first grant us faith. He gives us faith to believe.

What do we need to believe in order to be saved? Simply this: that though we were once utterly dead in our sin, God sent his Son to live obediently and to die shamefully in our place. Then he raised him from the dead, and, after forty days, Jesus ascended into heaven as the glorified God-Man. We have to believe that we can't earn our salvation but that he's done everything necessary for it. And none of us will believe that unless God grants us faith.

But what is faith? It's more than mere knowledge or even the agreement that such knowledge is probably true. It is trust. Saving faith is a *distrust* in our own ability to earn God's favor coupled with a *trust* that Jesus has done everything necessary to ensure our salvation, and that he offers it freely to us out of love.

Sometimes doubt grows because we've been confused about the nature of true faith and think that we should be able to move mountains with our words. What do you think Jesus meant when he talked about "mustard seed faith"? Do you trust that Jesus has done what you cannot do and that he is strong enough to save you? Then you have faith. If not, spend time talking with a trusted pastor or friend.

Truth 35: Saving faith isn't showy or outwardly powerful.

Truth 36: Saving faith is a childlike trust that Jesus is able to save you.

Your Heavenly Father Knows You

*"For the Gentiles seek after all these things, and your heavenly
Father knows that you need them all." (Matt. 6:32)*

BEING THE WORLD'S foremost heart-knower, Jesus understood that even on our best days most of us struggle with the
feeling that something bad is about to happen. A friend of mine
once described her experience as the incessant race to stay one
step ahead of the doom that threatened to overtake her. Jesus
understood that concern. He knew that we were worriers.

In the Sermon on the Mount, Jesus spent a significant amount
of time describing the problem that we have with worry. He talked
about the focus of our worries, their sources, and their solution.

We're thinking about worry today because our seeds of
doubt spring forth into weeds of worry and anxiety. We worry
because we try in vain to look into the future and have trouble
believing that God's got this whole mess exactly where he wants
it. We doubt his wisdom, his power, and his love. We think that
our plans are better and that we're wiser than he is—though we
would never say that. Or perhaps we doubt his ability to work
powerfully on our behalf—because, after all, if he could work in
our situation, why wouldn't he? Of course, at the bottom of all
these questions is the most terrifying one of all: Does he really
love? Does he really love *me*?

In response to our worry, Jesus offers something far more
helpful than a mere "Just say no!" He tells us that when we ask
questions of daily life, such as "What are we going to eat?" or
"What are we going to wear?" or any of the gazillion other doubt-
filled questions that we ask, we are thinking like homeless children who have been left destitute by a deadbeat dad and deserted

to find their way alone. He tells us that the reason we worry is because we have "little faith" (Matt. 6:30). We worry because we don't believe he's as good as he says he is. But then again, Jesus doesn't just say, "Stop it!" Instead, he reassures us that "your heavenly Father knows . . . " (Matt. 6:32). The one thing we must count on is that our Father is a good Father. He knows us, and he knows our needs. He will take care of us.

Your heavenly Father is no deadbeat, loser dad. He hasn't broken his vows, deserted his family, or left us to fend for ourselves. No, actually, he is watching over all his creation, even down to the most insignificant wildflower in the meadow or the dime-a-dozen birds that wing over our heads in the spring. You are his child. He is your Father. He has promised that he knows what you need and will care for you because he loves you.

Take time now to read Matthew 6:25–34. What does Jesus promise? What is his prescription for handling your worry? Why would he say that we should focus on his kingdom (not our own) and his righteousness (not on own)? What does verse 34 mean? Make a list of your worries, decide which ones you need to take action on, and then pray with thanksgiving for it all. Ask the Lord for faith to believe that he is a good and loving Father.

Truth 37: Worry is a by-product of doubt.

Truth 38: Our Father in heaven knows, provides for, and loves his children.

DAY 20

You Are Loved

*But God shows his love for us in that while we were
still sinners, Christ died for us. (Rom. 5:8)*

WE LEFT OUR discussion of doubt and worry yesterday
with a glorious proclamation: *God is your heavenly Father, and he
loves you.*

How did that statement strike you? If you're like me, you
might find it hard to believe. Perhaps, like me, you have never
known the constant love of an earthly father, so believing in a
loving heavenly Father feels foreign, uncomfortable. Perhaps
your father wasn't absent, but you wish he had been, because
he was anything but loving. Or perhaps, like me, you feel that
you haven't made enough progress in your Christian life to merit
God's ongoing love, even if he did forgive you for the sins you
committed before you came to faith.

Maybe once it was easy to believe that your heavenly Father
loved you, but then you went through troubles in your family or
church, or you faced devastating loss of health or material pos-
sessions, and now you're asking, "Do you *really* love me? Can I
really count on you?" I understand those questions. I, too, have
doubted. *Does he really love me? Is he truly that good? Aren't I too
damaged, too much of a mess, too doubting?*

In Romans 5, Paul has furnished answers to each of these
questions. He begins by reassuring us that God is at peace with us.
Our sin no longer separates us, because we are counted justified.
Simply put, *justification* means that we are not only completely
forgiven but also completely righteous. He can remain our loving
heavenly Father because in his sight we have a record of perfect
obedience.

In light of his ongoing love, we can be assured that our sufferings are not due to his anger with us but that they are at work to produce within us strong, hope-drenched character, because through them we taste his love. Our sufferings are given to us for the express purpose of deepening our faith.

In verses 6–10, Paul describes the sort of people God loves to save: he calls us "weak" (v. 6), "sinners" (v. 8), "enemies" who deserved "wrath" (vv. 9–10), those who made necessary "the death of his Son" (v. 10). Paul was never one to mince words. He wasn't concerned that we might get our feelings hurt. He knew he had good news, but he also knew that the only way for us to rejoice in the reconciliation God has brought was for us to hear the bad news first.

After reading Romans 5:1–11, answer the following questions:

- Why does Paul want to talk about peace with God?
- Why would we not have peace with him?
- Why does God allow suffering in our lives? Does this suffering mean that he is a wicked father or that he is punishing us? How can you know?
- How does Paul describe those whom God loves?
- What does it mean to be reconciled to God?
- How can we know that we are saved? What has God done to ensure that outcome?

Truth 39: We will always struggle with doubt if we think that God's love is based on anything we do.

Truth 40: The fact of our justification means that God has promised to be our loving heavenly Father forever—no matter what.

DAY 21

Silencing the Accuser

"Behold, I have taken your iniquity away from you, and I will clothe you with pure vestments." (Zech. 3:4)

YESTERDAY I SAID that justification means both forgiveness of sins as well as a record of perfect obedience. Justification means not only "Just as if I had never sinned" but also "Just as if I had always obeyed." What amazingly good news this is! Especially to doubters like us!

A story in the Old Testament perfectly illustrates our justification. It's found in Zechariah 3. In a vision, the prophet Zechariah sees a high priest named Joshua[1] who is standing before the Lord. Next to him is Satan, whose name in Hebrew actually means "the accuser." Before Satan even opens his mouth to point out Joshua's obvious faults, the Lord rebukes him, declaring that Joshua is a chosen one whom he personally saved.

This is a shocking scene, primarily because Joshua was wearing filthy garments in heaven. That word *filthy* actually refers to excrement—a vile portrayal indeed of Joshua's sinfulness. At the Lord's command, Joshua's disgusting clothes are taken away from him, and he is clothed with "pure vestments," including a clean turban.

Can you see how Joshua the high priest received justification on that day? His sin, depicted as dung-covered clothing, is removed from him. But that's not all that happened to him. He wasn't merely cleansed. He was also given holy clothing that assured him of his righteous standing before the Lord. Here's how another prophet, Isaiah, described the joy at his justification: "I will greatly rejoice in the LORD; my soul shall exult in my God, for he has clothed me with the garments of salvation; he has covered me with the robe of righteousness, as a bridegroom decks himself like a priest with a beautiful headdress, and as a bride adorns herself with jewels" (Isa. 61:10).

Satan's mouth was shut before he even tried to bring accusation against the one the Lord had chosen to love. All the filth that defiled Joshua was removed, and beautiful, clean clothing covered his nakedness and shame. In the same way, your justification means that you are both forgiven and counted holy. You are a beautifully clothed priest now (see 1 Peter 2:5, 9), ministering in prayer and praise before the throne of the King, who is also your loving heavenly Father.

It's important for you to rest in the reality of your justification, because the accuser will constantly remind you of your failures and of God's demands for holiness. His accusation will breed joy-depleting doubt in your heart.

Read Zechariah 3. Describe the events in this heavenly courtroom. Who is present? What does Satan want to do? Why do you think that Satan is named Accuser (see also Rev. 12:9–10)? What is Joshua's problem? How does the Lord solve it? In what ways has Satan accused you and denigrated God's promises in the gospel? What does the word *justification* mean? How does Zechariah's vision illustrate this New Testament truth? How does this passage describe those who are part of God's royal priesthood now (see 1 Peter 2:5, 9)?

Truth 41: Just as he did at the beginning of time, Satan continues to inject doubt about God into our hearts.

Truth 42: Your standing before God is not made up of your great faith or even your great works. It is made up of the righteousness of Christ alone.

DAY 22

Counted Righteous . . . Yes, You

*It will be counted to us who believe in him who raised from the
dead Jesus our Lord, who was delivered up for our trespasses
and raised for our justification. (Rom. 4:24–25)*

SOMETIMES IT'S HARD to keep believing. There are things I
have been waiting for and praying about for years. Looking back,
I see I have waited and prayed and waited and given up on praying and waited and prayed again, over and over, for nearly five
decades.

I'll also admit that, though I've tried to pray faithfully, I am
usually shocked when God answers my prayers. Recently that happened in my personal life in two different areas. I was as surprised
as anyone when God finally moved. And, even though I have seen
him answer recently, right now our family is facing another time of
need and I'm back to praying, waiting, and struggling with doubt
again.

Abraham and Sarah had awaited the birth of their promised
son for twenty-five years. Twenty-five years. They didn't have the
Scriptures. They didn't have a temple or church to worship in.
They were basically on their own. But they had an even bigger
problem: their biological clocks were not ticking anymore—they
had completely stopped. How could the Lord fulfill his promise?
I find it amazing that they continued to believe at all.

Abraham's faith, vacillating though it was, was good enough
for God. Even though there were times when he doubted, there
were other times when "Abraham believed God," and for that he
was called righteous (Rom. 4:3). It was by faith *alone*, not by his
works, that God, who "justifies the ungodly," counted him as righteous, holy, obedient (v. 5). Abraham wasn't living in a delusion.

He "considered his own body, which was as good as dead," and "the barrenness of Sarah's womb" (v. 19), and yet he continued, sometimes weakly, other times strongly, to be convinced that God was able to "do what he had promised" (v. 21).

Here's where we come in. Astoundingly, these words about Abraham's faith-righteousness were written not for Abraham's sake alone, but for ours also. God's righteousness is bestowed on us because we *believe* in "him who raised from the dead Jesus our Lord, who was delivered up for our trespasses and raised for our justification" (vv. 24–25).

The soul-comforting truth that works to quiet our doubt is simply this: If you have believed that Jesus died for your sins and was raised from death, then you are justified. If you believe, though only partially, then you are forgiven and counted righteous. Period. Remember that the record of Abraham's vacillating faith is written for your sake. He was counted righteous because he believed. Never perfectly, never consistently, yet still righteous.

What have you been praying about for years? Have you ever seen God answer prayer? Do you find that you, too, sometimes pray without really believing that God will answer? Why? Read Romans 4 and ask the Lord to enable you to believe that you are forgiven and counted righteous even though your faith isn't consistent.

Truth 43: Sometimes doubts spring up because we've been awaiting an answer for a long time.

Truth 44: If Abraham's wavering faith was strong enough to justify him, yours is, too.

ENDURING TRIALS
AND SUFFERING

DAY 23

How Long, O Lord? Forever?

How long, O LORD? Will you forget me forever? How long
will you hide your face from me? How long must I take counsel
in my soul and have sorrow in my heart all the day? How
long shall my enemy be exalted over me? (Ps. 13:1–2)

IN POURING OUT his heart to God, David describes what
seems like a bottomless well filled with brokenness and despair.
He is drowning in sorrow. Time drags interminably on. *Forever.*
He feels like God has forgotten him. He's having trouble remembering a time when he didn't feel this way. In fact, he's beginning
to wonder if God is really there or not.

In this psalm, David feels deserted and forgotten by God. But
has God actually deserted or forgotten him? Of course not. We
know that he hasn't, because other passages (that are not poetic,
emotional song lyrics like the Psalms) assure us that God never
forgets his people. For instance, Isaiah 49:15–16 tells us that
he never will, because we are "engraved" on the "palms of [his]
hands."

Even in the midst of despair, David remembered that he
couldn't trust his feelings. That's why he had to remind himself
daily of the truth. He said that he had to "take counsel" (Ps. 13:2)
in his soul. In other words, he had to tell himself what was true
and how his feelings lied to him. He was fighting to walk by faith
and not by sight.

What were the truths that David needed to remember? He
needed to remember God's steadfast love and his salvation (see
v. 5). He needed to remember that the Lord had "dealt bounti-
fully" with him (v. 6). He needed to encourage himself that there
had once been a time when he trusted, rejoiced, and sang—and,

because of that, he probably would again. He told himself to look back, to try to remember the days before this despair had overtaken him, and to base today's faith on yesterday's songs.

A common experience among those who doubt is a feeling of being forgotten. It's as though God has turned his back on us and trials are sure to stretch on before us *forever*. Compounding this bleakness is the suspicion that God sees our doubt and is disappointed because of it. Let's take direction from David and seek to counsel ourselves. Look up the following verses to see what their truth tells you about the Lord, and write it on index cards to keep with you. Whenever you're tempted to give in to the thought that says, "God—if there even is a God—has forgotten me. He's going to hide from me and give me over to those who hate me forever," remind yourself of these passages:

- Psalm 27:10
- Isaiah 49:15–16
- Romans 8:37–39
- Hebrews 13:5–6

Truth 45: When we're in a trial or filled with doubt, it's easy for us to forget God's goodness and to exaggerate our troubles.

Truth 46: No matter how bleak things look, we can counsel ourselves with the truth. God hasn't forgotten us.

DAY 24

A Divine Work of Art

Count it all joy, my brothers, when you meet trials of various kinds . . .
that you may be perfect and complete, lacking in nothing. (James 1:2, 4)

A YOUNG MOTHER discovered that she had breast cancer just a few months after her little girl was diagnosed with leukemia. A boy with Down syndrome suddenly lost his dad, causing him to weep uncontrollably in the foyer of the church. A beloved grandmother died while undergoing a relatively "safe" procedure. Each of these circumstances occurred during the last few months in my own church. Each of the people involved were believers. They loved God just like you do. They wanted to be well, to live, and to serve the Lord. If there were ever any reason for doubt, the problem of pain certainly qualifies.

I'm sure you have thought this: *If there really is a God, and he really is all-powerful, all-wise, all-seeing, and loving, then why does he allow people to suffer?* To these questions come answers that seem logical: *Perhaps he isn't powerful, wise, omniscient, or loving—or, worse yet, perhaps he isn't at all.* To our logic, allowing pain never corresponds to wisdom, awareness, power, or love. After all, if God could stop something bad from happening, why wouldn't he?

Many Christian philosophers and theologians have sought answers to these questions. In *The Problem of Pain*, C. S. Lewis wrote that the reason we struggle with these questions is because we believe that pain-free lives are far preferable to lives of suffering. I agree. If you offered me a life of pain or a life of pleasure, I'd take pleasure every time. Wouldn't you? But Lewis writes that, in bringing suffering into our lives, God creates a masterpiece fit for glory that would not be possible if he left us to enjoy only pleasure. "We are, not metaphorically but in very truth, a Divine work of art, something that God is making, and therefore something with which He will not be satisfied until it has a certain character. . . . In the same way, it is natural for us to wish that God had designed for us a less glorious and less arduous destiny; but then we are wishing not for more love but for less."[1]

A toddler will never understand why she can't have a second ice cream cone. And so she cries. But, as she matures, she'll begin to see that it is love that causes her mother to refuse to give her what she wants. That's what James is getting at when he writes that suffering changes us. It matures us. It teaches us that we can endure. And it makes us "perfect and complete." The Lord who loves us is after something more in our lives than our pleasure in the here and now. He wants to perfect us. That's going to hurt—but it doesn't mean that he doesn't love.

I'm not saying that pain isn't painful or that we shouldn't alleviate it. But there are times when we've done all that we can do, and yet the suffering continues. It's in those dark moments that we are most tempted to doubt God's love for us. Ask the Lord for wisdom to believe.

Truth 47: In the life of the Christian, suffering has meaning.

Truth 48: Suffering isn't a sign of God's disinterest or displeasure; it is just the opposite.

DAY 25

But the Lord . . .

At my first defense no one came to stand by me, but all deserted me. . . .
But the Lord stood by me and strengthened me. (2 Tim. 4:16–17)

THE APOSTLE PAUL knew what it was to suffer. He describes his ministry experiences with heartbreaking terms: "afflictions, hardships, calamities, beatings, imprisonments . . . sleepless nights [and] hunger" (2 Cor. 6:4–5). He had been slandered, dishonored, and treated as an imposter (see v. 8). And then, after all this suffering, Paul was sent to Rome again, where he had to stand before Caesar on trial for his life. He was alone. This is a man who had poured out his life for the building up of the church; we have to wonder where his friends were. He writes that everyone "deserted" him—that no one stood by him.

It's easy to assume that Christians ought to act better. They should be truer, more faithful friends. They should stand up for those whom they love and not desert them in their hour of need. And they shouldn't stab them in the back. I have spent nearly five decades worshipping and working in churches with other Christians. And, while I've known many lovely people, one thing is for certain: Christians rarely act like Christians.

Since Jesus said that the identifying mark of a believer is the love that he has for others (see John 13:35), there have been times when I've wondered whether there really were any Christians at all. And I'll admit, with shame, that there have been plenty of times through the years when I was the one doing the deserting—although of course, at the time, I would feel completely justified. Let's face it—no one deserts his friend because he thinks that desertion is an admirable activity. We think that we're doing the right thing. Fortunately for all of us, there is a friend who "sticks closer than a brother" (Prov. 18:24).

Paul's testimony was that during his time of need, when all his friends deserted him, the Lord stood with him; he came to him and comforted him. The Lord is good at comforting those who have been wounded by their brothers and sisters, because he knows what it's like to face suffering alone. In his greatest hour of need, while he writhed in agony in Gethsemane, his dearest friends, Peter, James, and John, gave in to their desire to sleep. At his trial before the Sanhedrin and a Roman tribunal, Jesus stood alone, while Peter swore (with an oath) that he didn't even know him. And Jesus knows what it is to be stripped and hung up on a cross to die. He did that alone, too. Jesus knows what it is to come "to his own" and to have them refuse to "receive him" (John 1:11). He even knows what it is to be deserted by his Father (see Matt. 27:46).

Can you trace some of the doubt you are experiencing to the actions of other Christians? Describe the situation. In what way does Paul's or Jesus's experience of being deserted or betrayed comfort you? What do you think Paul meant when he said that the Lord stood by him and strengthened him? Describe a time when you knew that the Lord was helping you. Spend time in prayer, asking the Lord to give you the grace to believe that he's with you right now.

Truth 49: It's easy to think that Christianity isn't true when fellow believers fail to love as they should.

Truth 50: The Lord will stand by us and strengthen us even when our friends fail us.

DAY 26

Consider Him

*For consider the one who endured such hostility by
sinners against himself, so that you will not grow weary
in your souls and give up. (Heb. 12:3 LEB)*

JESUS'S EARTHLY LIFE speaks powerfully to his commitment
to bring us to himself—to assure us of his love. The mere fact that
the second person of the Trinity, God the Son, was formed as an
embryo in a girl's body, to be born in the humblest of circumstances, foreshadowed the life he had chosen to live. He chose life
as a human being with lineage that could be traced, with a beating
heart, seeing eyes, and aching feet, so that we would know that
we have something more than mere myth without foundation.
He chose to suffer. This is no fairy tale. This is verifiable fact. And,
yet, we forget—we struggle to remain in the faith. Day after day
we need reminding.

The Lord knows how weak we are, how hard it is for us to
continue to believe. "He knows our frame; he remembers that we
are dust" (Ps. 103:14). What are we? Mere dust trying to believe.
Jesus chose to suffer so that, when we wonder if we really are
loved, we have a sure answer.

Look at his life. Read the Gospels. "Consider him who
endured from sinners such hostility against himself, so that you
may not grow weary or fainthearted" (Heb. 12:3). Think about
him. Consider how, "for the joy that was set before him," he
"endured the cross," thinking nothing of the "shame" that his public execution announced. Why would he subject himself to such
disgrace? Why not appeal to his Father, who would "at once" send
him more than twelve legions of angels (Matt. 26:53)? Because
he knew we would need more than pious platitudes uttered from

the top of a high mountain by some self-proclaimed holy man. We needed a Savior who would get dirty. We needed a God who would bleed, a Messiah who would die right before our eyes. And so, in order to prove that he was who he said he was, he offered himself in our place. He fulfilled prophecy. He cried out, "My God, my God, why have you forsaken me?" (Matt. 27:46).

Consider Jesus. Consider how he died. This cry testified to the God-forsakenness he experienced. At any moment during those final excruciating hours, he could have stopped it all. Yet, even when he searched in vain for his Father's smiling countenance, he continued on. He quoted Scripture and fulfilled prophecy. He refused to take up the power that was rightfully his. You needed proof. He provided it. He knows what it is to be bewildered. He knows what it is to fail to understand, to feel completely alone.

Reread the verse that opened this day. In what ways have you grown weary or been tempted to give up? How does your doubt play in to your experience of weakness? How often do you "consider" Jesus and what he has done to provide a sure foundation for your faith? Read the stories of his birth (see Matt. 1:18–2:18) and death (see Matt. 26–27:54). How would considering him like this build your faith and help you avoid feeling like you should just give up?

Truth 51: There is enough historical proof surrounding the life and death of Jesus of Nazareth to dispel reasonable doubt.

Truth 52: Jesus knows what it's like to struggle for assurance. He did so on the cross, for your assurance.

I Believe, Help My Unbelief

"But if you can do anything, have compassion on us and help us." And Jesus said to him, "'If you can'! All things are possible for one who believes." Immediately the father of the child cried out and said, "I believe; help my unbelief!" (Mark 9:22)

MARK 9 IS about the faith of four different groups of people. It opens with Jesus taking three of his disciples up a high mountain, where they witness him revealing the true nature of his glory to them. Shining and transfigured, he converses with two long-dead heroes of faith: Moses and Elijah. You would think that, after an experience like that, they'd have a stalwart faith that would never doubt. But they don't.

Next we're introduced to the rest of the disciples, who are arguing with a group of scribes. The disciples have tried unsuccessfully to cast a demon out of a boy. Although we're not told what they are arguing about, it's a pretty safe bet that the disciples are trying to figure out why they have been unsuccessful, while the scribes (who didn't believe in miracles) are probably telling them to just give it up.

And finally we're introduced to a desperate father and his beloved, demon-possessed, only son. "Teacher," he says, "I brought my son to you [but you were gone] . . . So I asked your disciples to cast it out, and they were not able" (vv. 17–18). After seeing the convulsing child, Jesus asks the father, "How long has this been happening to him?" "From childhood," he answers. "But if you *can* do anything, have compassion on us and help us" (vv. 21–22).

"If you *can!*" Jesus responds. "All things are possible for one who believes" (v. 23).

This poor father has been disappointed more than once. He's begun to doubt that what he has asked is even possible. But Jesus's heart is not only filled with compassion but also full of power. He assures the father that, because Jesus truly believes, he can accomplish anything. The father mistakenly thinks it's his own faith that's in question, so he cries, "I believe; help my unbelief!" (v. 24) The father assumes that his son's ongoing suffering is caused by his own lack of faith. Sometimes we can feel that way, too. But, rather than giving up, he asks Jesus for help. How does Jesus respond to his confession of unbelief? How does he respond to questions about his ability and love? He heals the boy. He "took him by the hand and lifted him up, and he arose" (v. 27).

There are times when we wonder about God's ability to help us. We ask "If you can" questions. Has that happened to you? Then there are other times when we know that we doubt. Those are the times when we say, "Help my unbelief." There are still other times when we question the Lord's willingness to help (see Mark 1:40–41). How does Jesus respond to pleas for compassion, help, and faith? He gives us what we need. That doesn't mean that we always get what we're hoping for, but our questioning and unbelief don't put him off. He loves to guide and help us. He will strengthen our faith. What do you need today? Ask him.

Truth 53: Sometimes we doubt God's power, and at other times we doubt his love or willingness to help.

Truth 54: Jesus won't chide us for questioning his compassion or power or for asking for faith to believe.

DAY 28

Wait for the Lord!

I believe that I shall look upon the goodness of the LORD *in the land of the living! Wait for the* LORD*; be strong, and let your heart take courage; wait for the* LORD*! (Ps. 27:13)*

KING DAVID, though he was beloved by God, lived through many years of trial. As the youngest of seven sons, he was given all the jobs that the older brothers didn't want. Did the sheep need tending? Did the older boys need a food delivery while they warred against Goliath's armies? David was their boy. Even after he was anointed king, he spent years running from Saul. It would be easy to assume that once he became king, his life got easier. But that's not the case. Aside from his own personal failures, he faced enemies outside the nation and within his own household. David was "a man after [God's] own heart" (1 Sam. 13:14). He knew that he was "the apple"—the center—of God's eye (Ps. 17:8). He was beloved by God. And yet . . .

In Psalm 27, David recounts the troubles he's facing. In his fight to overcome his fears, he reminds himself about the Lord's faithfulness: The Lord is his light, salvation, and stronghold. He believes that the Lord will hide him from trouble; he will lift him up. He prays that the Lord will be near him. He utters a poignantly sad prayer of desertion: "For my father and my mother have forsaken me" (v. 10). Although we don't know which of David's many trials initiated this song, we know that in addition to being deserted by his parents, he was being attacked by "evildoers," "adversaries and foes," "an army," "enemies," and "false witnesses" (vv. 2–3, 6, 11–12).

What does David teach us about how to respond when we face trials of various sorts—when it seems that everyone is against us and even our family and best friends turn away from us? When I have faced difficulties like this, it's been easy for me to doubt, to try to run away and hide, to question God's goodness.

But David approaches his problems with this helpful method. First, he cries to the Lord. He prays for help to continue to believe, to continue to trust. He tells himself that he will be confident no matter what (see v. 3). He sets his heart on the Lord in order to "gaze upon" his "beauty" (v. 4). He sings and prays to him (see vv. 6–7). And when the Lord commands him to seek him, his heart responds, "Your face, LORD, do I seek" (v. 8). As he continues to pray for deliverance, he believes that he will "look upon the goodness of the LORD in the land of the living!" (v. 13). And then he does one more thing: he waits. He waits for the Lord to answer. He encourages himself to be strong. And he waits.

Read Psalm 27. List all the words that David uses to describe his enemies. Now, what words does he use to describe God's care for him? What would it mean for you to "seek" the Lord's face? What is beautiful about the Lord that can help you in your time of trial? In your context, what would waiting look like? What steps can you take to demonstrate your faith (weak though it may be) while you await God's help?

> **Truth 55:** Acknowledging that we are in a time of trial isn't contrary to praying in faith.
>
> **Truth 56:** The passage of time is frequently the hardest part of belief, and yet God frequently delays in order to strengthen our faith and patience.

BE OF GOOD COURAGE

DAY 29

The Father Himself Loves You

*"For the Father himself loves you, because you have loved me
and have believed that I came from God." (John 16:27)*

I SPENT MY childhood longing for a father. You see, aside from a few infrequent visits during my elementary-school summers, my biological dad was absent. A stepfather did try (unsuccessfully) to take his place, but by the time I was twelve, he was gone too. Now, as a woman in her twilight years, I can testify that one dominant motivating desire in my life has been to know the love of a father, and this craving has caused me much despair and doubt.

But in 1971, I heard the good news from my friend Julie that there was a forgiving Father after all, who actually did love me and claimed me as his own. Although that news completely altered the trajectory of my life, I have still struggled with trusting in his love. I would like to say I have faithfully trusted every day for the last forty-six years, but that wouldn't be true. Sure, there are days when I really do believe (and don't doubt), but there are also seasons when I doubt that he loves me . . . and when I can't see any reason why he would.

As Jesus ate his final Passover meal with his friends, he told them this wonderful truth: "Because you have believed the truth about who I am, and because you have loved me, my Father loves you." It would be easy to think, *Well, of course the Father loves them—after all, they're the apostles!* But if you made that assumption, you'd rob yourself of this precious truth: the Father didn't love them because of the great things they were going to do, or even because their love was so strong or constant. Don't forget that, within hours, they had all deserted him and one had denied even knowing him. Later, after the resurrection, we never hear

Jesus withdrawing this assurance: if you believe (even weakly) that Jesus came from God, and if you love him (yes, weakly), the Father, who knows how hard it is for you to continue to walk by faith and not by sight, loves you.

The sad truth is that many of us grew up without a dad. But even those who have fathers in the home may never hear that they are loved or forgiven. And, of course, even those who had a good dad never had a perfect one. There is only one good Father! The great news is that if you believe that Jesus is his Son, and if you love him (though weakly), this good Father has pledged to love you and never walk out.

Do you have trouble believing that? Of course you do! I do too. So why not spend time now in prayer, asking God to help you believe and to remind you of his faithful love? Then make a list of the ways you have been driven by longing for a father's forgiveness and love. Can you see any sinful patterns in your life that were expressions of this desire? Is there anything you need to do (such as confessing sin, asking forgiveness, or making restitution) as you seek to rest in this Father's love?

> **Truth 57:** Everyone, but especially those with absent or less-than-gracious fathers, has trouble believing that a good Father loves and forgives them.
>
> **Truth 58:** God's love for us is based not on the strength of our faith or on the constancy of our love but on the goodness of his Son.

DAY 30

Who Shall Separate Us from the Love of Christ?

Who shall separate us from the love of Christ? . . . For I am
sure that neither death nor life, nor angels nor rulers, nor things
present nor things to come, nor powers, nor height nor depth, nor
anything else in all creation, will be able to separate us from the
love of God in Christ Jesus our Lord. (Rom. 8:35, 38–39)

DEAR DOUBTING FRIEND, *nothing* can separate you from
God's love. Even death, the definitive divider, isn't strong enough
to wrench you from his grip. No, he will be there to lovingly guide
you to your resting place in paradise. No matter how long you
live, you can't outlive his love. No supernatural being, no demonic
angel or power, nothing in this present world or the world to come,
nothing from high above or deep beneath—in fact, *nothing in all
creation*—can separate you from God's forgiving, pursuing, faithful, sustaining, gracious love. Not even the weakness of your faith,
the inconstancy of your love, or your failure to live a completely
successful Christian life can sever you from his devotion to you.
"There is absolutely nothing that can ever drive a wedge between
the children of God and their Heavenly Father."[1] Nothing.

Again, it's easy to think that Paul was so confident because
he was, well, the great apostle Paul. But let me remind you that
this wonderful passage comes right on the heels of Romans 7,
which, as we saw on day 15, doesn't present a glowing testimony
of Paul's perfect victory over sin. No, Paul wasn't convinced of the
constancy of God's love due to the power of his own perfect life.
He was convinced because he had had a face-to-face encounter
with the risen Lord—and when a formerly dead person knocks
you off your horse and blinds you, you don't need more proof.

Despite his ongoing struggle and trials, Paul writes that the steadfastness of God's love is a fact of which he is convinced. He says, "I am sure"—meaning that he is utterly convinced, completely persuaded.

But how does the testimony of a man from the first century help us? I'm sure that none of my readers have ever had a Damascus Road confrontation with the resurrected Jesus or spoken personally to Paul. But we don't need to. We have been given the reliable testimony of a real historical figure who so believed the message he was preaching that he lived a life of hardship and died a martyr's death. In a courtroom, that testimony would be referred to as credible, believable. Remember, too, that Paul wasn't the only one who died in service of this great love.

Will you believe Paul's beautiful declaration of the love of God in Christ for you? I'm sure that you want to. If you're still struggling to believe, it might be helpful for you to reread Paul's conversion stories in Acts 9; 22:6–16; and Galatians 1:11–17. Paul gave up a hard-earned reputation and a lucrative resume because he witnessed a convincing truth. And this truth was that, though he had been exterminating Christians, God loved him and had work for him to do. How would your life change if you were convinced of God's love for you? What sorts of things might you do today if you knew that you were loved? Why not pick out one or two of them and proceed as if the assumption were true?

Truth 59: Nothing can separate us from God's love.

Truth 60: The testimony of the early church should be enough to convince us of the constancy of God's love for us.

DAY 31

Finally Free from Doubt

We know that while we are at home in the body we are away from the Lord, for we walk by faith, and not by sight. (2 Cor. 5:6–7)

PAUL WANTS US to be "of good courage," because a day is coming when we will be away from the body, which seems scary—but we will also finally be "at home" with the Lord (2 Cor. 5:8). Right now our hearts may still be prone to doubt—to that unsureness, hesitancy, or indecision that we're having trouble shedding. But rather than looking inward, at the weakness of our faith, we're to look ahead—to focus our thoughts and faith on the day that is surely coming, when our faith will be sight. One day we will know the assurance that Job spoke of when he said, "For I *know* that my Redeemer lives, and at the last he will stand upon the earth. And after my skin has been thus destroyed, yet in my flesh I *shall see* God, whom I shall see for myself, and my eyes shall behold" (Job 19:25–27).

Think of that. Job had lost everything. His skin was rotting off his body, and his children were rotting in the grave. He had nothing—not even the Bible or the assurance that is ours because of Calvary. And yet he was able to look forward and say that he "knew" that there was a Redeemer and that one day he would see him. What a glorious work of the Spirit in his life!

Yet, even though Job been given insight when he declared this, he still faced numerous days of doubting and questioning until the Lord finally delivered him. On the day of his deliverance, he said, "I had heard of you by the hearing of the ear, but now my eye sees you" (Job 42:5). Of course, even then, Job was speaking by faith. Throughout those long, arduous days of doubt and despair, as Job wrestled with everything that he thought he knew about God, the Lord sustained him so that he came out the other side saying, "Now I see you" (see Job 42:5). But, even better, the wonderful reality is that Job isn't doubting or questioning any longer. He no longer has to speak or walk by faith. His belief that he would see his Redeemer has finally come true. He is at rest and completely filled with joy. His faith has become sight at last.

Now we have spent a whole month together . . . thinking about our doubts, considering people who doubted, and exploring the reasons why doubt is so common for us all. I trust that the Lord has used our time to build your faith and to help you focus on Jesus, who had perfect faith in your place.

Let me leave you with one more thought: a day is coming (and probably sooner than we know) when all our doubt will be banished and we will open our eyes to see what we have always longed to see—a loving heavenly Father and his blessed, loving Son.

The day is coming when all our doubt will seem like nothing more than tiny annoyances—and when the truth will be so strong and tangible, we'll be able to touch it. Rejoice. One day your faith will be sight.

Truth 61: Neither Job nor any other believer who has gone on to be with the Lord struggles with doubt now. And neither will you.

Truth 62: One day you will have perfect certainty.

Truths for Doubters

Truths about the Bible's Claims

Day 6: Logic and observation teach that all things come from other things and that all things have a beginning.

Day 6: There is an intelligent designer behind everything that was made, and we know him as Jesus Christ.

Day 7: The Bible makes claims about itself that set it apart from all other ancient books.

Day 7: There is enough evidence in the Bible's fulfilled prophecies to move someone from doubt to reasonable belief.

Day 8: Jesus claimed to be God. We know enough about his life to know that he wasn't crazy or a liar.

Day 8: Jesus fulfilled a number of specific prophecies over which he had no control.

Day 9: While Jesus might have tried for some unknown reason to fool people by fulfilling prophecies, he couldn't have done so from the cross.

Day 9: It would take more faith to believe that Jesus's claims to be God are just a hoax than to simply believe those claims.

Day 10: The disciples wouldn't have concocted a resurrection story. They were too busy hiding.

Day 10: The resurrection isn't a myth. It means that all that Jesus said and did and all that he set out to accomplish is true and reliable.

Day 26: There is enough historical proof surrounding the life and death of Jesus of Nazareth to dispel reasonable doubt.

Truths about Doubt

Day 1: Doubt has been around since the beginning.

Day 3: Sometimes doubt can make us respond foolishly.

Day 3: Having more physical proof, like bread falling from heaven, won't erase our doubt.

Day 11: One reason that you struggle with doubt may be the ease of the command "Believe."

Day 14: Doubt doesn't disqualify you from serving God's people.

Day 19: Worry is a by-product of doubt.

Day 21: Just as he did at the beginning of time, Satan continues to inject doubt about God into our hearts.

Day 22: Sometimes doubts spring up because we've been awaiting an answer for a long time.

Day 27: Sometimes we doubt God's power, and at other times we doubt his love or willingness to help.

Day 29: Everyone, but especially those with absent or less-than-gracious fathers, has trouble believing that a good Father loves and forgives them.

Day 31: Neither Job nor any other believer who has gone on to be with the Lord struggles with doubt now. And neither will you.

Truths about Faith

Day 2: It's foolish for us to compare the strength of our faith to the strength of others'.

Day 4: Faith doesn't demand complete certitude, even in the face of death.

Day 5: Certainty in faith isn't consistent. Everyone questions truth that they were once assured of.

Day 11: Even though the command to believe appears too easy, the truth is that it is too hard. Only God can grant you saving faith.

Day 18: Saving faith isn't showy or outwardly powerful.

Day 18: Saving faith is a childlike trust that Jesus is able to save you.

Day 21: Your standing before God is not made up of your great faith or even your great works. It is made up of the righteousness of Christ alone.

Day 31: One day you will have perfect certainty.

Truths about God's Love

Day 1: God loves and saves doubters.

Day 5: Jesus boasted about John even when John doubted him. He doesn't shame doubters; he gives them evidence to rebuild their faith.

Day 16: The story of "doubting Thomas" is actually the story of a reassuring Jesus.

Day 16: Jesus continues to be willing (and able) to answer all your questions.

Day 19: Our Father in heaven knows, provides for, and loves his children.

Day 20: We will always struggle with doubt if we think that God's love is based on anything we do.

Day 20: The fact of our justification means that God has promised to be our loving heavenly Father forever—no matter what.

Day 27: Jesus won't chide us for questioning his compassion or power or for asking for faith to believe.

Day 29: God's love for us is based not on the strength of our faith or on the constancy of our love but on the goodness of his Son.

Day 30: The testimony of the early church should be enough to convince us of the constancy of God's love for us.

Day 30: Nothing can separate us from God's love.

Truths about God's People

Day 2: Every child of faith, even the "great" ones, had times of significant doubt.

Day 4: Even doubters can stand in faith courageously.

Day 14: God uses people who have both times of faith and times of doubt. People are qualified to lead God's people by Jesus, not by the strength of their faith.

Day 15: Not even the great apostle Paul lived a life worthy of salvation.

Day 22: If Abraham's wavering faith was strong enough to justify him, yours is, too.

Truths about Our Trials

Day 23: When we're in a trial or filled with doubt, it's easy for us to forget God's goodness and to exaggerate our troubles.

Day 23: No matter how bleak things look, we can counsel ourselves with the truth. God hasn't forgotten us.

Day 24: In the life of the Christian, suffering has meaning.

Day 24: Suffering isn't a sign of God's disinterest or displeasure; it is just the opposite.

Day 25: It's easy to think that Christianity isn't true when fellow believers fail to love as they should.

Day 25: The Lord will stand by us and strengthen us even when our friends fail us.

Day 26: Jesus knows what it's like to struggle for assurance. He did so on the cross, for your assurance.

Day 28: Acknowledging that we are in a time of trial isn't contrary to praying in faith.

Day 28: The passage of time is frequently the hardest part of belief, and yet God frequently delays in order to strengthen our faith and patience.

Truths about Sin and Salvation

Day 12: God's mercy extends even to the most terrible sinners who are sorry for their sin.

Day 12: Your sin might be "ever before you" in your own eyes, but it isn't in God's.

Day 13: Jesus, not the correctness of their prayer or the zeal of their service, saves sinners.

Day 13: No matter how long you've waited or how much time you've wasted, Jesus loves enough to forgive and rescue.

Day 15: Freedom from condemnation is not primarily a feeling. It's a verdict that has been pronounced from outside you.

Day 17: The apostle Paul abused and murdered Christians, and yet Jesus forgave and used him.

Day 17: Sometimes the failure you are most ashamed of is the very thing that the Lord will use to prove his great mercy.

Notes

Tips for Reading This Devotional

1. Jonathan Leeman, *Reverberation: How God's Word Brings Light, Freedom, and Action to His People* (Chicago: Moody, 2011), 19.

Introduction

1. Of course, there are certain philosophies that posit that there really aren't any realities, but we won't bother with that foolishness. Those kinds of philosophies may work well in academia, but they're useless when we come up against the fears and pains and experiences of our everyday lives.

Day 7: The Reliable Word

1. See Don Stewart, "Does the Bible Claim to Be the Word of God?" Blue Letter Bible, accessed June 20, 2018, https://www.blueletter bible.org/faq/don_stewart/don_stewart_276.cfm.

2. There are forty main contributors to the Bible—thirty in the Old Testament and ten in the New (see "FAQ #2: Who Wrote the Bible?" Biblica, accessed June 20, 2018, https://www.biblica.com /resources/bible-faqs/who-wrote-the-bible/).

3. See "The Cyrus Cylinder," Collection Online, The British Museum, accessed June 20, 2018, http://www.britishmuseum.org/research /collection_online/collection_object_details.aspx?objectId=327 188&partId=1.

4. See Hugh Ross, "Fulfilled Prophecy: Evidence for the Reliability of the Bible," Reasons to Believe, August 22, 2003, http://www .reasons.org/explore/blogs/todays-new-reason-to-believe/read /tnrtb/2003/08/22/fulfilled-prophecy-evidence-for-the-reliability -of-the-bible.

5. See Don Stewart, "Does the Bible Claim to Be the Word of God?" Blue Letter Bible, accessed June 20, 2018, https://www.blueletter bible.org/faq/don_stewart/don_stewart_276.cfm; Sid Litke, "Is the Bible Reliable?—Seven Questions," Bible.org, accessed July 13, 2018, https://bible.org/article/bible-reliable—seven-questions; Hugh Ross, "Fulfilled Prophecy: Evidence for the Reliability of

the Bible," Reasons to Believe, August 22, 2003, http://www
.reasons.org/explore/blogs/todays-new-reason-to-believe/read
/tnrtb/2003/08/22/fulfilled-prophecy-evidence-for-the-reliability
-of-the-bible; and Stand to Reason at http://www.str.org.

Day 8: All This Took Place to Fulfill

1. See Mary Fairchild, "Old Testament Prophecies of Jesus," ThoughtCo, updated May 3, 2018, https://www.thoughtco.com /prophecies-of-jesus-fulfilled-700159.

Day 14: The Faithful Shepherd

1. See Jon Ronson, "How One Stupid Tweet Blew Up Justine Sacco's Life," *The New York Times Magazine*, February 12, 2015, https:// www.nytimes.com/2015/02/15/magazine/how-one-stupid -tweet-ruined-justine-saccos-life.html.

Day 16: Doubting Disciples

1. We also know that Thomas continued to believe (see Acts 1:13).

Day 21: Silencing the Accuser

1. Not to be confused with the political and military leader who lead the people of Israel into Canaan and who has a book named after him.

Day 24: A Divine Work of Art

1. C. S. Lewis, *The Problem of Pain* (1940; repr., San Francisco: Harper San Francisco, 2015), 34–35.

Day 30: Who Shall Separate Us from the Love of Christ?

1. Robert H. Mounce, *Romans*, The New American Commentary 27 (Nashville: Broadman & Holman, 1995), 192.

BIBLICAL
COUNSELING
COALITION

The Biblical Counseling Coalition (BCC) is passionate about enhancing and advancing biblical counseling globally. We accomplish this through broadcasting, connecting, and collaborating.

Broadcasting promotes gospel-centered biblical counseling ministries and resources to bring hope and healing to hurting people around the world. We promote biblical counseling in a number of ways: through our *15:14* podcast, website (biblicalcounselingcoalition.org), partner ministry, conference attendance, and personal relationships.

Connecting biblical counselors and biblical counseling ministries is a central component of the BCC. The BCC was founded by leaders in the biblical counseling movement who saw the need for and the power behind building a strong global network of biblical counselors. We introduce individuals and ministries to one another to establish gospel-centered relationships.

Collaboration is the natural outgrowth of our connecting efforts. We truly believe that biblical counselors and ministries can accomplish more by working together. The BCC Confessional Statement, which is a clear and comprehensive definition of biblical counseling, was created through the cooperative effort of over thirty leading biblical counselors. The BCC has also published a three-part series of multi-contributor works that bring theological wisdom and practical expertise to pastors, church leaders, counseling practitioners, and students. Each year we are able to facilitate the production of numerous resources, including books, articles, videos, audio resources, and a host of other helps for biblical counselors. Working together allows us to provide robust resources and develop best practices in biblical counseling so that we can hone the ministry of soul care in the church.

To learn more about the BCC, visit biblicalcounselingcoalition.org.